Leasing 101 - Garden Style

Robert Starnes

Anniversary Edition

The Multifamily Housing Guide

Leasing 101
Garden Style

Have you ever wanted to become a Leasing and Marketing Professional in the Multifamily Housing Industry? Well, now you will have all the tools you need to excel as a top Leasing and Marketing Professional.

Robert Starnes

Leasing 101 - Garden Style

Published by Starnes Books LLC

ISBN: 978-1-7325803-1-2 (sc)
ISBN: 978-1-7325803-2-9 (e)

Printed in the United States of America
First Printing 2016
Library of Congress Control Number: 2016917301

Revised Edition Printed 2018

Contents

Leasing 101 - Garden Style

Introduction

Have you ever wanted to work in the Multifamily Housing Industry? If you said yes, then this is the book for you. Becoming an effective Leasing and Marketing Professional is only the first step. This guide will give you the tools I did not have when I started my career in this industry.

My goal is to help structure our industry by giving a little bit of my leasing knowledge to everyone who is interested in beginning a career as a Leasing and Marketing Professional or anyone who may want a refresher guide to get back to the basics of the Leasing and Marketing Professionals' intricate role in this amazing industry.

I have been in the Multifamily Housing Industry for many years. I have worked for a few of the nation's largest management companies. I have over ten years with just one of those companies. I started as a Leasing Professional myself, back in 2000 with no previous experience. Back then there were no books on how to lease apartments, or even what was expected of me as a Leasing Professional, so I was on my own to find out.

While in search of a new career, I found a temporary-employment service that specialized in the Multifamily Housing Industry. The temporary service gave me a one-day training in fair housing and a one-day crash course on how to show an apartment. Needless to say, I did not have much to rely on. Within three months of working as a temp at the first community I was assigned to, I was hired as a full-time employee with the management company. From my first day arriving at the community, I knew this was the career for me. Since my time as a temporary Leasing Professional, I have held several positions and worked in several states.

I worked my way up from a Leasing Professional to an Assistant Manager, to a traveling Manager, to an on-site Manager, and to a Multisite Manager. No matter what position I hold, I always know leasing is, and always will be, number one.

Chapter 1

Time to Open

When is the best time to get to work? Do you arrive right on time, or do you get there a bit early? Well, we are going to go over opening the clubhouse.

It is usually best to arrive at work at least fifteen minutes early each day. You will need that time to open the clubhouse, fitness center, business center (or any other amenity your property may offer), and model or show homes (do you have keys?) and to walk the path you will be taking for on-site tours that day. If your office opens at 9:00 a.m., you should be ready to answer the phones, greet people coming in, and even show an apartment at 9:00 a.m. No one likes to come into an office and have to wait while you finish opening before he or she is helped. (Golf cart users, see Key Points to Remember at the end of the chapter.)

Does your desk have brochures and price sheets ready for the day? What about printed layouts you can give to your guests? Do you have them ready in your desk? Not every property will use a price sheet or even brochures, but whatever you use, are they ready at your desk? Does your company require you to fill out a guest card, or do you fill one out online? If you use paper guest cards, do you have plenty for the day? You want to make sure your desk is stocked!

Whether you have a large or small clubhouse, you want it to look and smell fresh when you open. Make sure that there is no trash lying out around the desk, you have guest cards ready, iPads or other devices you may use are charged up, drinks and snack stations are fully stocked, and computers are on and ready for the day. If your property has an opening checklist, use it. If your property does not have one, make one. Do what you can to make the morning easier for you. You can locate examples of a price sheet and opening checklist in the appendix.

If your community has a twenty-four-hour fitness center, business center, media room, resident sitting area, pool, spa, or any other amenity, make sure they are clean and ready to use. The fitness center should be in order, and if you have free weights, make sure they are not on the floor but in their proper places. Make sure the radio or TV is on (not too loud). Clean off the equipment if it looks dirty. Make sure you have cups for the water-cooler and that the wipes holder for the fitness equipment is filled. This is also the time to check the restrooms. Are they clean? Do they have paper towels, soap, and tissue paper? Make the fitness center a place where residents will want to work out. If it has a sauna and you supply towels for guests, are there plenty available for them? By now, you should have the picture of how the amenities should always look: like new and properly functioning.

Now that the clubhouse and amenities are looking their best, it's time to open the model or show homes. While you are walking to open the model or models, you have the perfect opportunity to make sure your walking path is clean. If you see trash, pick it up. If the area is heavily trashed, alert the maintenance team; this could be something they did not know about or are already on their way to clean. If the path cannot be cleaned, find a new path. Do not have a tour path that is not clean. You get only one chance to make a first impression, and trust me, you do not want it to be perceived as the trashy place. You want people to remember you and the property in a positive way.

You have walked your path, it is looking good, and you've reached the model. When you open the door to the model or show home, what is the first thing you notice? Does it smell funny? Are there any lights out? Is it dirty? Again, this is the first impression of your apartment home, make it count. If you see a leak, alert a member of the maintenance team. If you only have one model or show home, it will need to be repaired quickly. If you have other homes to show, then let maintenance know of the issue and move on to the next one. Let's say there were no leaks and no lights out, and it smells great and is ready for viewing. Then what do you do? You walk back to the office, checking your tour path one more time, so you can start the day.

Key Points to Remember

- Arrive at least fifteen minutes early each morning.
- Make sure clubhouse and amenities are clean and ready to use.
- Make sure your tour path is clean and clear of all trash.
- Make sure the model is fresh and ready for viewing.
- Be ready to start leasing or answer the phones promptly at opening time.
- Make sure the golf cart is clean and ready for you to use for the day.
- Make sure to use proper golf card etiquette, no speeding, slow down for speed bumps, and make sure everyone is on before moving.

Chapter 2

The Perfect Call

It may not seem like much, but the right way to answer a phone may make all the difference in someone leasing an apartment from you. This section will give a few examples of how to answer the phone, prequalify potential new neighbors, set appointments, and have a perfect phone call.

The goal of a great phone call is to get the potential new neighbors to visit you and the community. Getting them there is the hardest part! Once you have an appointment set, most of your leasing work is done. How do you achieve a perfect phone call? Utilizing a phone card as a guideline will ensure that you get all the important information that you need, including name and contact information, as well as all the information regarding exactly what your prospect is looking for in his or her next home!

Leasing 101 - Garden Style

A perfect phone call is as easy as asking all the right questions. A phone card will list the following information that you should get:

- name
- phone number
- e-mail address
- preferred way of contact
- how they heard about the property
- when they are looking to move in
- what size apartment home they are looking for
- their budget for housing, if they have one
- how many people will be residing in the apartment home
- how many people will be over eighteen (this age varies depending on your state and company policy)
- whether they have any pets
- whether they have a floor preference
- anything specific they are looking for or require in their new home

The card should also remind you to do the following:

- Describe your property amenities.
- Discuss the benefits of living at your community and the management company.
- Discuss local area attractions.

- *Set an appointment.*
- Ask if they need directions to your community.

A friendly reminder: if you have not asked all the above questions, you will not have all the tools you need for success. How can you follow up with your guest if you failed to get his or her name, phone number, or e-mail address? A sample phone card can be located the appendix.

Before you pick up a ringing phone, make sure that you are truly available to take the call. If you are working on a file, stop and put all your attention on the opportunity that is calling you! If you are working with a resident or future neighbor already, it's best not to answer the phone. Doing so will not make you look as if you are avoiding a call; it will look like you are there for the person in front of you. You will want the person on the other end of the ringing phone to feel the same way. If you have to get the phone, make sure you can excuse yourself to take the call, and then either ask the caller if you can put him or her on hold, or call back when you are available. Wait for the reply and then take the necessary steps for placing the caller on hold or hanging up. Do not leave callers on hold for very long; they may lose interest in you and the community or think, *Is this how they treat all their guests or residents?*

Leasing 101 - Garden Style

Here is an example of a proper way to conduct the perfect phone call.

You: Thank you for calling Learning Apartments. My name is Sam. How may I help you today?

Caller: *Hello, Sam. I am looking for a two-bedroom apartment for the end of May. Do you have any available?*

You: Yes, we do. May I ask who I'm speaking with?

Caller: *My name is Brenda.*

You: Nice to meet you, Brenda. Do you mind if I ask you a few questions about what you are looking for in your new home?

Caller: *Yes, that would be fine.*

You: Great! May I get a telephone number for you, in case we get disconnected?

Caller: *Yes, it is (555) 214-1212.*

You: How about an e-mail address? That way I can send you a link to our website or updates on our homes here.

Caller: *Sure, it's brenda@my.com.*

You: Now, how do you prefer to be contacted?

Caller: *E-mail.*

You: Perfect. Now, how did you hear about Learning Apartments?

Caller: *I was just looking on the Internet.*

You: Do you remember which site? We like to keep information on which sites work best for our new neighbors.

Caller: *I just googled apartments in this area.*

You: Okay, great. Now, you said you were looking for a two-bedroom for the end of May. May I ask how many people will be staying in the apartment home?

Caller: *Three.*

You: How many are over the age of eighteen [nineteen depending on the state]?

Caller: *It will be my husband, me, and our six-year-old daughter.*

You: Do you have a budget you wanted to stay within?

Caller: *Yes, around $1,100–1,300 a month.*

You: Do you have a preference for first, second, or third floor?

Caller: *Is there a price difference between the floors?*

You: Yes, the first floors are a bit higher, because they have wood flooring.

Caller: *Okay, then no preference.*

You: Will you be brining any pets with you? [Make sure you know your pet policies, breed restrictions, weight limits, pet fees, deposits, pet rent, etc. Once you have their pet info, you can continue with the call.]

You: Is there anything specific you are looking for in your next apartment home?

Caller: *Yes, I must have a washer and dryer in the apartment.*

You: Now that I have a clear picture of what you are needing, I can better assist you. We have a spacious two-bedroom, two-bath, on the second floor available for the end of May. This particular apartment home has been recently renovated and comes with stainless steel appliances, granite countertops, brushed nickel light fixtures, dark cherry cabinets, and a washer and dryer. [This is where you will paint a picture of what you have that is closest to their needs. Describe the apartment in detail and don't leave anything out. They may have called, or will be calling, other communities, and you want to make sure yours stands out to them.] How does that sound?

Caller: *Great!*

You: A few more things about our community. We are managed by Learning Apartments, Inc., and we are one of the largest management companies in the nation. We offer twenty-four-hour emergency lock-out services and on-site maintenance. With our transfer policy and being nationwide, you can transfer to any of our properties, and your application is pre-approved. [This is where you want to let them know about the company you work for.]

You: Here at Learning Apartments, we have a resort style pool with spa, twenty-four-hour fitness center with a dry sauna and free weights, limited access gates, free covered park, and valet trash from your front door five days a week. [This is where you will describe the amenities you have to offer.]

[Avoid security questions, unless your community offers security and you are permitted to say so per your company policies. Try to encourage callers to contact the local police department if they want to know about crime in an area.]

You: Do you currently live or work in the area? When you would like to come in to view one of our fantastic apartment homes? Do you prefer morning or evening? I have a 10:00 a.m. or 4:30 p.m. available for today. Which is best for you? [You want to give them an option either morning or evening; that way you are creating urgency for the appointment.] I want to make sure you see this particular apartment home, because it is the last one we have available.

[Don't stretch the truth or lie about being the last one, unless it is the last one of that price, layout, or floor preference. You want to avoid any issues that may lead to a discrimination allegation with US Department of Housing and Urban Development, simply because you were trying to lease the apartment. You may have other unit types like that particular one, but it may not be on the same level, have the same exposure, flooring, or interior features.]

You: Do you need directions to Learning Apartments?

[Now that you have everything you need from them, repeat it back to them.]

You: Perfect, Brenda. I have you scheduled for today at 3:00 p.m., to view one of our two-bedroom apartments for move-in the end of May. Is that correct?

Caller: *Yes, that is correct.*

You: Now, are there any other questions you may have that I did not cover? If you think of anything, please feel free to call or e-mail me; I am here to answer any questions you may have. You will be receiving an e-mail to confirm our appointment today at 3:00 p.m. I look forward to meeting you, Brenda. Thank you for calling Learning Apartments.

Now that you have established a rapport with the caller, you can make the calls a little more personal by adding humor or relatable topics. I like to add things such as the following:

- "Now, I will give you a call if I don't see you by our appointment time, to check whether you are not either lost or need to reschedule."
- I like to relate to them if they have pets, I will ask their pets name and age. Then I can talk about my dog, Julie. This will make them feel more comfortable about a pet-friendly community.
- If they discuss that they like to grill out, I will let them know that I love grilling, but I'm not very good at it, so I have no problem sampling food anytime someone is grilling. I joke that they need to make sure if they are going to use the grills, it's a day that I'm working!

Make it feel and sound natural when you are speaking to the caller.

Another important note: some callers simply want to know what the prices are, or what specials you are offering. You want to lead the conversation so you may obtain the necessary information to help determine what you have available to meet their needs, but you don't want to frustrate them either. It's easy to get discouraged and allow them to lead the conversation, but you need to control the call. Let them know you will be happy to get that information to them, but you will need a few more details from them in order to provide them the correct rates.

Practice makes perfect, so don't avoid a ringing phone, answer it when you are able to, not while you are with a guest! Every time you answer a ringing phone is an opportunity for you to possibly have a new neighbor at your community. Put on your smile and be yourself! It's time to shine!

Key Points to Remember

- Smile when you answer a phone.
- Ask all the questions on a phone card.
- Paint vivid pictures; because it is a phone call, this will help the caller remember you and the community.
- Set an appointment for all guests to view your community.

Chapter 3

The Perfect On-Site Tour

Now that you have mastered the perfect phone call, it's time to learn what comes next: the on-site tour!

If you have truly mastered the perfect phone call, then most of your work is already complete. You should have almost everything you need when your appointment arrives. You know what they are looking for, when they need it, any preferences, and when they are going to be there.

When your appointment arrives, make sure your work desk or leasing area is clean and tidy. You will only get one chance to make a positive first impression, so make it count! You will want to make sure you greet your guests as soon as they come in. Stand up, greet them as you are walking to them, offer a hand shake, and then offer them something to drink, either from the coffee bar or refreshments you may have. Make sure you offer everyone the same refreshments. Now it's time to finish inputting their information into the system you use for storing guest information. Do *not* make photo copies of IDs until either the application is approved (or at time of application), or at move-in (check with your company and state policies). You will need to check their IDs so you can verify it's the same person you made an appointment with, and to get the rest of their information (date of birth, ID number, current address, whether it is current and not expired). Most companies require some proof of identification that is current and government issued, so no Sam's Club cards, student IDs, or expired driver's licenses. Check with your company policy in regard to holding the ID or giving it back to the guest after the information is recorded on the guest card; each company is different. Some required IDs from all guests that are being taken on a tour, and they hold the IDs in the office until after the tour for safety reasons. Some companies may require at least one ID of anyone over the legal age, and they'll give it back to the person before the tour. You already have all their information on the guest card, so holding the ID is unnecessary in my opinion. Check with your company and state policy.

Your guest card is filled, the IDs are either put away for holding in a secure place or given back to the guest, and you are ready to go on tour.

Since you arrived to work fifteen minutes early, you already know your tour path is clean and the amenities are fresh for viewing. You leave the clubhouse, keys in hand for show homes, and you know where you are going. As you are walking to the first stop of your tour, let's say it's the fitness center, start describing it to them. You want guests to get a clear picture in their mind before you arrive. Once you are there, you can show them around and explain the hours and policies about the fitness center. If you know one of their main desired amenities is the fitness center, then spend a little more time there so they can start feeling at home and seeing themselves working out there.

As you are leaving the first stop to the next amenity (still with a freshly walked path from this morning), start describing the next stop to them. Your property may not have many amenities, so you will want to make sure you make each one count. Continue with each amenity on your tour until you reach the show home. If there is an area on the tour path that may leave some awkward silences between you and the guest, fill in that area with a little more about the management company, local attractions, restaurants in the area, or the closest mall. Try to remember what they said during the phone call, and make the conversation fit their needs. You don't want to talk about the new steakhouse to vegetarians, would you? Make this tour about them and their needs and wants for their next home.

Now that you have arrived to your show apartment home with your guest, open the door to the fresh and clean show home, and let the guest in first. One closing tool you can try is to give the keys to the guest and allow them to unlock and open the door. This gives them a sense of coming home. You will always want to keep yourself between the guest and the exit. This is mainly for your benefit for safety, but it also lets the guest get the view of the home first. You can still lead a conversation without being directly in front of the guests. You want them to walk around and get cozy. As they are walking around and looking at the show home, talk about features the home offers them. Again, remember what they are looking for, have you been listening to them? Here are some examples of leading the conversation without being in front of the guests.

- "Here, as you walk in, you can see the large living room. You may notice the dining room is separate from the living room. Since you said you like to cook and entertain, will your dining room furniture fit here?"

- "I remember you said you must have a large kitchen. As you can see, you have plenty of counter and cabinet space in this kitchen. You have the open bar area that is great for entertaining guest. How would you set up this kitchen?"

- "As you are about to walk into the bedroom, you may notice that this is the perfect size for a king or queen size bed and furniture. What size bedroom furniture do you have?"

- "Now, don't forget to look in the spacious walk in closet. You said you had to have plenty of space for your shoes. Well, you now will have all the space you need with this apartment home!"

- "The best part about having a washer and dryer in this home is you do not have to go to a laundry facility to do your laundry. You are able to go straight from the dryer to the closet!"

These are just a few ways to lead the tour without getting their way, so guests can get the feel for the home. It also keeps you between them and the door.

Some guests will have objections to the layout you are showing. Don't worry; the objections are another way for you to overcome them and close the deal. They might not have the vision you have for that layout and simply need a little help placing their furniture.

Here are a few objections you may come across, and some ways to overcome them.

Guest: *I didn't like the washer and dryer on the patio.*

You: Well, the best part about the washer and dryer being on the patio is that you don't have to listen to them while you are watching TV or cooking dinner!

Leasing 101 - Garden Style

Guest: *I don't like the bathroom is in the bedroom.*

You: [Comical] For me, if someone is coming over to visit me, then I tell them they can just use their bathroom before coming over to my place. [Practical] I love my bathroom in my bedroom, so if I do have guests staying over on the couch, I don't have to wake them or cover up if I need to use it in the middle of the night. Or, this would give you a reason to make sure you room is always clean when you do have guest coming over.

[Factual] Well, the great thing about the bathroom in the bedroom is that if you need to use it in the middle of the night, you don't have far to go. Or, I would rather have the restroom in my bedroom instead of right off the living room, so if people need to use it, they don't have to be uncomfortable using it, thinking everyone can hear them.

Those are just some of the objections you will hear. Overcoming an objection is also another way of showing you care about your neighbors. You want them to be happy there. You may have seen residents' apartments of the same layout, and you remember how they set up their apartments. It is up to you to be quick with a way to overcome objections. An easy way to be more prepared for the objections you hear on your property is to take yourself on a tour of your property.

What do you see that you may not like? If you see it, then bet someone else will see it too. How would you overcome your own objection? Think like a guest, not a leasing professional. Do some things there outweigh the other things for you? Can you deal with a small living room if you get a garden tub and walk in closet that you really love?

Now that you have toured the property and show units, is time to go back to the clubhouse and close the deal. As you walk back to the office, summarize what guests said they were looking for and what you have to meet their needs. You will also want to create a sense of urgency because you want them to lease today. Here are some examples of what I've used to get the lease.

You: So, what do you think so far? It does not take much to lock in that apartment today. All I need is for you to let me know which is easier for you, as well as a paper application, or you can fill out one online. I can have you approved in the same day.

You: Let's go in so I can get you my card and the information on what I have available today. Our homes lease quickly here, and I don't want you to miss out on the one we discussed on our tour.

You: All you have to do to secure that home is to fill out the application and pay the application and reservation fee. How would you prefer to pay today, check or credit card?

Here are a few examples of creating the sense of urgency.

You: I have two homes available, but only one of them has everything you are looking for.

You: With this one having the pool view, it will not last long, and I don't want you to miss out.

You: These rates and specials are only good for a short time, because our rates change daily. The price today could be more tomorrow for the same home!

Remember: don't lie to the guest to create urgency. You may have ten vacant apartments to rent, but out of those ten, how many meet their needs? Now you have gone from ten to maybe two available homes for them.

Not everyone will come back to the office and lease right after your tour, so don't get discouraged. You will get more Nos than Yeses. The industry standard in multifamily housing is closing 33 percent of your tours. That means if the first tour says no, you have two more for the day that may say yes.

Even though the standard is a 33 percent closing ratio, who wants to be standard? Set goals for yourself that are a bit higher so that you can push yourself. Aim for breaking company records with most leases.

Many people think that they are just a leasing professional. Well, I'm here to tell you there is no such thing as *just*. The Leasing and Marketing Professionals are on the largest stage of any property management company. Every position for the office staff is being a leasing professional first and foremost. Here is a prime example of what I mean by this.

On my first day at a new property, the office was very busy. While everyone in the office was with a guest, someone came in and started helping us out. She was very nice, and the office staff seemed to know her. It was my first day, so as far as I knew, she was part of the office team. When she walked in again, we were all busy with guest. Instead of going to the manager's office or trying to avoid the guest, she walked up to the next guest waiting and asked if she could help them. She proceeded to ask me for our price sheets, layouts, and keys to the model, and then she went back to the guest and filled out their guest card to go on tour. When she returned, she looked like she had worked at that property for years. I found out later she had been to the property only a few times. Needless to say, the guests she toured leased from her right then and there. As things slowed down in the office, she was introduced to me as the Regional Vice President. That was when I knew my position as a leasing consultant was very important and came first, no matter what title or position I had.

Over the years, I have seen many Leasing and Marketing Professionals waste so much time worrying about what the other staff members are doing, or how they handle their workloads. Many of them say, "I could do better than them," when they have not even mastered their current position. Don't waste your energy or time trying to get a promotion when you have yet to master your current position. Think about how that energy could be used to think of new ways to overcome objections, or ways to generate traffic.

Being a Leasing and Marketing Professional is more than just leasing an apartment; it is learning how to read your guests, listen to what they want or need, and having them want to lease from you not just because of the apartment home but also because of you!

Key Points to Remember

- Your desk or leasing area is clean of all clutter.
- You only have one chance to make a good first impression.
- Treat everyone who walks into the leasing office the exact same way.
- Always, always, always ask for the money.
- Stay focused on your current position.
- Set your goals to be above the standard.

Chapter 4

The Application

In order to process an application, it would be best if you read the application first. This way you will be able to answer any questions your guest may have while they are filling out their application. Also, find out what the application criteria is for your property, and what your company deems as grounds for denial.

Knowing what makes a complete application will help you in the long run. What all do you need from the applicant before you can screen them? Do you need proof of income? Do you get a copy of their ID at the time of application? Do you need any fees? Do you only accept online applications, or does your property only accept paper applications? Find out what your company accepts and requires, so you can be prepared when someone is ready to lease from you.

No matter what type of application you can accept, the concept of a completed application is the same.

1. You want to make sure the application is completely filled out. An application will require name, current and previous address, date of birth, social security number, (government-issued ID number), employment information, other occupants, and much more. We will go through the key points of an application to remember.

2. Having checked to make sure the application is complete will make the screening process faster, if you do not have to contact the applicant for information that is missing.

3. Look over the application and make sure it is filled out completely and signed. Follow your company policies. Do you have the proof of income that you will be using? The application fee(s), deposit (if required), reservation fee (admin fee), and copy of Government ID? (Except Military ID's, those are illegal to copy)

Now that you have either the paper or online application, you want to make sure you have collected the fees that go along with the application (application fee, reservation fee, or deposit). Also make sure you have their proof of income. *Never go by what people put on their applications as their income.* You have a formula you use, or maybe an income calculation sheet, so their incomes may be different than what you calculate.

The average week in a month is calculated by taking 52 weeks in a year and dividing it by 12 months in a year: 52 weeks / 12 months = 4.33 weeks in a month. Instead of just having 4 weeks in a month, you actually have an average of 4.33 weeks in a month. Then, 33 percent would be a third of their monthly income. You will always want to refer to your company's guidelines for what income percent they require.

The weekly income would be used if someone gives you proof he has a weekly salary, or in some cases, receives overtime every week and wants to use that to increase his monthly income. On the weekly example, if someone shows proof of income, and it shows he makes $600 a week, regardless of the number of hours worked, he qualifies for a rent amount of $857 per month ($600 w × 4.33 wm = $2,598 monthly income; $2,598 mi × 0.33 = $857.34).

In the hourly example, if someone shows proof of income, and it shows she makes $12 an hour and works 40 hours a week, she would qualify for a rent amount of $686 per month ($12 × 40 h = $480 a week income (w); $480 w × 4.33 wm = $2,078 monthly income; $2,078 mi × 0.33 = $685.87).

The example income sheet, located in the appendix, will show you an easy way to use the above formula to use the weekly income or hourly rate to verify what rent people qualify for. You will see if you want to change the percentage of income required to meet your property's needs, simply change the 33 percent at the top to the percentage your property requires (i.e., 3.25 times the rent would be 35%; 2.5 times the rent would be 40%).

Find out your policy on students and applicants who do not meet income requirements. Some companies may allow for students, which do not qualify with their income, to have a guarantor/cosigner (someone who is signing the lease, but not reside there, that will be held financially responsible for the rent, if the lease holder falls behind); find out your company policy on this. In most cases, the guarantor may have to be a relative or family member in the United States, and they may have to make five to six times the rent. That means if the rent is $600 a month for the student, the guarantor may have to make $3,000–3,600 a month. This is to insure they make enough to cover their own bills as well as the rent, if the student falls behind. Make sure you find out if a guarantor is accepted for just the apartment home or per applicant. For example, two students apply, and neither qualifies with income; do they need one guarantor, or will they both need a guarantor? This could change the amount the guarantor has to make monthly to qualify. In other words, if only one is needed, then the guarantor would have to qualify for five to six times the full rent, whereas if each one has to have a guarantor, then each guarantor would only have to qualify for five to six times the rent each student is responsible for.

Income seems to always be where Leasing and Marketing Professionals mess up. Using the income sheet in this book will make it easier for everyone to get the same outcome with the same proof of income.

This is a good time to give your applicant a welcome letter. The welcome letter is such a great tool to use; not only does it give your new applicant a sense of approval, but it also works at a receipt of what they have paid (i.e., application fees, reservation or redecorating fee, security deposit) and has their new address on it, as well as important numbers to call to set up their utilities. If you provide this to them before they leave, you can tell them that this will be their new address and the amount that they will need to bring at move-in, once you have approved them. This will keep them from having to come back in later to get their address from you. The welcome letter also helps find any errors you may have before you are ready to type the lease. If your welcome letter is correct, and you are off when their final approval comes back, then anyone in the office can pull the file, look at the welcome letter, and be able to know what you offered. This will keep everyone on the same page.

A welcome letter (which you can find an example of in the appendix) is the best way to assure you have all the correct information regarding a move-in. You may already have one for your property, so you simply need to know where it is and know how to prepare it.

Now that applicants have their welcome letter and you have the income figured out, as well as all documents needed to screen the applicant, let's get started. Make sure you have a log-in to the program you screen, though, and also ensure all the information from the application matches what you have in your property software (e.g., Yardi, Onsite, RentRoll, Entrata, MRI). How you screen applicants will determine where you need to input their information. If you screen through your property software, then you will want to make sure it is all correct in that system. If you use a separate company to screen applicants (SafeRent, First Advantage, OneSite), then you will want to make sure you correctly input the information.

Now that everything on the application has been checked and entered into your property screening system, it's time to proceed. Make sure you know what the policy is for non-US residents. Do you have a supplemental application and the supporting documents that are required? How do you proceed with the screening process? Do you know where to send the information? Remember that you want to get the applicant approved as soon as possible, so know what to do.

The application criteria and the applicant screening results will affect how the application is approved. Do you know what to do next? Does the screening company you use have conditions with the approval? I've seen approved, approved with conditions, and denied. Conditions could be from additional deposits, to certified funds only. Denials should match your grounds for denial. Check with your company for all application criteria and the grounds for denial before proceeding with the application screening.

Now that that application screening has come back, what are the conditions, if any? Do they have to pay a higher deposit? Can they only pay with certified funds (cashier's check or money order)? Once you have the answers, you will either correct their welcome letter to reflect the conditions. If they are approved with no additional conditions (per company policy for approval), then it's time to call and let your applicants know of their approval. You can let them know their current welcome letter is all they need until the move-in date, or you can state that you have a new one for them, with their conditions, to sign.

Congratulations, you have just changed an applicant to a future resident!

Key Points to Remember

- The application is completely filled out.
- Income has been verified and has supporting calculation sheet.
- Collect all applicable application fees.
- Create a welcome letter.
- Call your applicants once they are approved.

Chapter 5

The Applicant File

Preparing an applicant file is important, and it is easy to complete. I will take you through a few steps to ensure your applicant file is perfect and ready for approval.

You have a completely filled in application, proof of income, payment for application, hold fees your company requires for new leases, and any other documents you are required to have. Before screening the applicant, where are you going to put those things? You will need a secure location in which to keep the files. Remember, an application has personally identifiable information on it (full name, previous last name, social security number, date of birth, and even driver's license number). All of this information could be used to steal someone's identity, and we do not want that information to fall into the wrong hands. Find out where these are kept while you're not working on the file.

What is the approval process for an applicant at your property or company? Does the manager have to approve the application documents before you can screen the applicants, or does the manager do a final approval after you have screened them? There is really no set industry standard to the final approval of an application, so it's best to find out from your manager.

I have learned in the past sixteen years that most applicant files are set up the same in industry norm. We will focus on the left side of the file folder for now. You will put anything that applies to the application, application process, application documents, and any type of correspondence between you and the applicant on the left side of the file folder—basically, anything that is not a legal part of the lease contract (which we will discuss later). Again, there is no industry standard for what order the left side of a file fold have to be in, but you will want to put them in the same order for each file.

Assuming you have everything you require from an applicant, it's time to put those items in a file. I have used the following placement order of documents for many years now, and it has worked well for me and my team members:

1) Copy of application fee / admin fee / deposit paid

2) Copy of Government issued Identification
3) Completed application with application criteria and grounds for denial
4) Proof of income with calculation sheet (signed by two team members)
5) Screening company results (approval or denial)
6) Manager's approval (before or after screening)
7) Welcome letter (signed by both parties)
8) Checklist with comments section

With this order, the bottom page will be the copies of the fees, and the top page will be the checklist with comments section. As you can see, there is no place order for a copy of a form of identification; the reason is that any copies of any form of identification should only be received after the final approval is complete, unless you have a supplemental application for non-US citizen that requires those documents in order to process the application. I like to get the ID copies at move-in, just so I don't have to have my new neighbors come only for making a copy for the file.

Let us keep in mind that the file you are about to create will be an extension of you. How do you want your team members to perceive your organizational skills? Are you sloppy or neat with the order? The applicant file should tell a short story to anyone who picks it up and may need to help while you are off. You will want anyone looking at the file that you created to know exactly what you have told the applicant and exactly where you are with the file. Are you waiting on something from the applicant, or are you just waiting on the manager's approval? A great file can save a lot of wasted time from looking through the file to find what the status is, and it may even let you avoid some awkward phone calls on your day off from your manager or other team members. Many companies have application checklist for files. If they do have one, use it!

Here are a few things an application checklist may have on it.

1) Leasing professional's name
2) Applicant's name
3) Applicant's phone number
4) Copy of the application fee, reservation fee, or deposit (check / money order / online)
a) Payment type, number, and amount
b) Hold fee type, number, and amount
5) The following items:
    a) _____ Completed application signed
    b) _____ Copy of Government ID
    c) _____ Criteria and grounds for denial
    d) _____ Proof of income and calculation
    e) _____ Has the applicant been screened
    f) _____ Approved/Denied
    g) _____ Welcome letter
6) Lease dates
7) Lease terms (how many months)

8) Rental rate
9) Any special offered
10) Final approval
11) Comments section

If your company does not utilize a checklist, you can create one yourself. This will only help you succeed as a leasing professional.

As I mentioned before, you want your file to tell to anyone who pulls it a story of that file. There are several reasons someone other than yourself may need to pull one of your files. You may be off one day, and the applicant may call to change their move-in date, or request another copy of the welcome letter be sent to them. By utilizing an applicant checklist, anyone can see what you have told the applicants, as well as what all you have sent them, or what you still need from the applicants. This can also help reduce misinformation to a future neighbor. If you do not put the rental rate you quoted them, and your rates change daily, then the team member who is trying to help may quote a new rate to them that could be higher or lower than what you quoted. That could become a big issue, so you want to avoid those types of misunderstandings.

When you are contacting the applicant, you should always document in the file with whom you spoke, the outcome of the call, and when you spoke to him or her. This should be done in every file, and it can be documented under the comments section of the checklist. This will ensure that anyone who pulls the file will be on the same page as you and the applicant. A neat file leaves little room for errors.

Companies and properties may have different ways to number the applicant files. Take the time to find out how they want them labeled and follow that policy. If you see that there is no set labeling system in place, ask if you can start one. One simple way to label an applicant file folder is the apartment number, layout type, and floor level. For example: "1015 B2, 1st floor." I would not put applicants' names on the label because they could be denied or cancel, and then you would have to create a new label for the next applicant. Making one file folder for each apartment on your property works great for me. If someone gives a notice to vacate, I can pull the files, remove all the lease and application information, and binder clip it and place it with the notice to vacate. Then I can put the empty apartment file back in the file cabinet. Once I have an application for that apartment, I can simply pull that apartment file, and I'm ready to go.

All you have to do is find what works best for you, your team, and your company's policies. After that, applicant files will be easy to convert into resident files!

Robert Starnes

Key Points to Remember

- An applicant file will be an extension of you; make it neat.
- Use an applicant checklist, or make one.
- Never get copies of IDs until final approval or move-in.
- Document the application file every time you speak to the applicant.
- Make one file folder for each apartment.
- Canceled application or denials should be pulled from file and given to the assistant manager for processing.

Chapter 6

How to Follow Up

We discussed that not every guest will lease, but we did not discuss why. There are many reasons someone may not lease. In this section, we will go over some of those reasons and what you do with those guest cards. We will learn why they are important and how to follow up.

There are several forms of communication that can be used as follow-up. You can send out a thank-you card or e-mail, or simply give people a call to thank them for visiting you. You should always perform some kind of thank-you follow-up on the same day of the tour. Make sure you are contacting them in the preferred way they mentioned during the tour.

The time frame you have for following up will vary, based on why they did not lease from you. You may have anywhere from three days to six months to follow up with someone. We will cover those reasons they did not lease and how to follow up based on those reasons.

Also, you may have paper guest cards or online guest cards. No matter what type of guest card you use, you will have different ways of keeping record of your follow-ups.

Keeping accurate information about all your guests is very important. The information you receive from your guests will help with your follow-up with them. Just because they do not lease today with you does not mean they will not lease in the future with you.

I encourage you to get a planner. A planner is a great way for you to keep up with when your guests need an apartment and when you should follow up with them. Many companies have some form of software that you are supposed to use to input all your traffic. Whatever software you have, learn it and use it to its full ability. I have seen many leasing professionals put the information in their system, but they never use it the way it was intended to be used. If you choose a written follow-up log to keep track of your guest, you can find a sample of each in the appendix.

One of the main reasons to follow up with your traffic is to get them to come back out and lease. Following up will increase your closing ratio and allow you to find out who has leased somewhere else so that you don't waste your time or theirs.

Let's go over a few reasons why someone may not lease from you on the first day you tour him or her. The following are just a few reasons someone does not lease on the same day as the tour:

- Future date needed (This means they are not looking for today and may be more than ninety days out.)

- Roommate or spouse needs to view (This is when one roommate comes to view the apartment first and he or she needs to bring the other party back if your community meets their needs.)

- Still looking (This would be someone who just started looking and you are his or her first stop, or you may have been his or her last stop and he or she is deciding on where to lease.)

- Viewing for a friend (You will have guests come in who are looking for a friend or a family member who may not be local.)

- Shopper (This would be guests who are there to do a mystery tour on someone at the property. This could be set up through the company you work for or even HUD. They will not say they are shoppers or give any other reason for not leasing, but it is still good to know what a shopper is.)

- Unqualified (This would be someone who will not qualify under your application criteria but still wants to view an apartment.)

- Apartment size or type unavailable (Someone is looking for a specific size or style layout that you do not have available during the time needed.)
- Unsure of move-in date (This would be someone who either is waiting on a job offer in the area or may be putting a house on the market.)

The reason someone gave you for not leasing will help determine how you will follow up with them. Let's use the following guest information to determine ways to follow up.

John Williams knows he will be moving to your area in the next six months for work, and he has starting looking for a place to live. During his tour with you, he prefers to be contacted via e-mail.

1. Send John an e-mail thanking him for touring with you on the same day.
2. Send John an e-mail twenty-four hours later letting him know that you will be there to help him if he has any questions, or if things change and he needs to move sooner.
3. Send John another e-mail after a week; this lets John know you are still there to help him.
4. John has confirmed that his date will not be any sooner. Now you can schedule your follow-ups with John on a monthly basis (the planner could be used here).

5. Send John an e-mail sixty days before his move date, letting him know what you may have available (many properties have a sixty-day notice, so you may have something for him to lease in advance).

6. E-mail John thirty days before his move-in date, creating the sense of urgency for him to lease from you.

You will continue with your follow-up either until he leases from you, or until he has informed you that he has leased elsewhere. If he has leased somewhere else, find out where and why.

You will use the same follow-up method for traffic two weeks out as you would for sixty days out. The only thing that would be different is the time between follow-up. Here is a breakdown of a follow-up time frame for different dates needed.

•   One week: A thank-you the same day, first follow-up after twenty-four hours, second follow-up after forty-eight hours, third and final follow-up after seventy-two hours. Make sure the final follow-up lets applicants know you will not be contact them anymore if they have not already told you they have leased elsewhere.

•   Two weeks: A thank-you the same day, first follow-up after twenty-four hours, second follow-up after forty-eight hours, third follow-up after one week, and fourth and final follow-up a couple of days before they need the apartment.

- One month: A thank-you the same day, first follow-up after twenty-four hours, second follow-up after forty-eight hours, third follow-up after one week, fourth after two weeks, fifth and final follow-up one week before the move-in date needed.

As you can see, the follow-ups for the first two days are the same for all traffic that did not lease. The reason for the first two days' follow-up is because you want to keep your property fresh on people's mind as soon as they leave. You may be the only property that has tried to follow up with them, which shows just how important they are to you. They feel needed by you and would want to feel that way at the next place they live.

The final follow-up is to let them know that because you have not had a response from them, you are going to assume they have found a place to live already, or their needs have changed, and you don't want to keep bothering them. In a way, you are going to be breaking up with them. I have found out that when you tell people that you are going to stop calling or e-mailing them, they will get back to you quickly. They don't want to be broken up with; they would rather do the breaking up. If they have not told you already they have leased elsewhere, then it's up to you to let them go or force them to let you know they are no longer interested.

Do not skip follow-up steps. Check with your company's policies and then follow up. Make sure you are following up with all your traffic in the same way. Do not give up if you have not heard back from them in a day or so; you never know what may be going on in people's lives that has kept them from getting back to you right away. Remember that they have a choice to lease somewhere, and you want them to lease with you!

Key Points to Remember

- A thank-you follow-up should be completed on the same day as they tour.
- The second follow-up should be completed twenty-four hours after their tour with you.
- Keep accurate records, either in a planner or the property software you are using.
- One of the main reasons for the follow-up is to get your guest to come back out to lease.
- Send a break-up e-mail after all attempts have had no response.

Chapter 7

Creating the Lease

Before you create a lease agreement, you should read one. Do you understand the lease agreement and addenda's? The lease is very important because the smallest mistake could cost the property and owner money. We will go over portions of a lease and things to know about a lease.

It is best if you have taken the time to print and read your lease agreement from front to back. If you have not done so already, you may want to have it available during this chapter.

The following are some key points to know about any lease:

- resident name
- address of apartment
- rent amount
- lease dates

- security deposit
- reletting fee
- number of days required for a notice to vacate
- what types of notices are accepted
- what day rent is due
- the late date and late fee
- insufficient funds fee
- where to pay rent
- early termination of lease policy
- number of days guest may stay before being added onto lease
- military clause
- community policies

We will go over these key points so you will learn how important each one is. This is not all you should know about a lease agreement, so we will go over other addendum's later in this chapter. For now, we want to focus on what people will ask you the most about a lease.

The majority of the key points are on the first page of a lease agreement. Some may have their own addenda's, which we will go over in this section.

I will breakdown how each of the key points could cost the property or owner if there is an error on them. It is very important to double-check the lease agreement before having it signed by either party. There will be some cases where an error was missed by all parties, but we will also learn how to quickly get those corrected.

Most communities and management companies require a sixty-day written notice to vacate (a set amount of days someone would have to give the office if they are not going to renew their lease, or if they intend to break their lease), depending on what the state allows. You will need to know the length of notice your state requires for an expiring lease, or one that has expired and is now a month-to-month lease. Some states will allow a property to request a thirty-day notice, which means if they are month-to-month, then they would be required to give a fifteen-day notice to vacate.

Here is a scenario with some incorrect areas on a lease agreement. I will explain how these errors can cost the property or the owner.

Scenario:

You have a typed lease for John Williams for apartment #717. He has now lived at the property for five months. He was approved with no security deposit. His rent is $1,250 a month. Rent is due on the first and is late after the third; on the fourth, a late fee of 10 percent of the rent will be charged to his account. His lease is a twelve-month lease starting January 1. A sixty-day written notice is required to terminate the lease early, or if the lease is expiring. The reletting fee is 85 percent of the rental rate, which would be $1,062.50. You require two months' rent as a termination fee, with a sixty-day written notice, if the lease is to be broken at any time during the lease or if he is not going to renewal the lease at the end.

Actual Lease Agreement Information

Name: John William
Address: 3215 W. Main Street #617
Lease Dates: 1/1/15–1/31/15
Rent: $1,050
Security Deposit: $1,000
Late Fee: $105
Notice to Vacate Days: blank
Early Termination Addendum: Amount $1,250
Resident is Late with rent: blank

Now, you will learn just how these small mistakes can be costly. Let's say Mr. Williams has not paid rent for the fifth month of residency. As you can see, Mr. Williams' name is misspelled: the lease shows Mr. William, and the *s* is missing from his last name. The manager sent him a legal notice for nonpayment of rent, and if the name is misspelled on the lease, then I bet it was misspelled on the notice. Now, I have actually been to court for an eviction that I filed for someone who had not paid rent in two months. Once in court, the resident pointed out that his name was misspelled, and the judge ruled in his favor. I had to go back to the property and put the correct spelling of his name on the notice of nonpayment of rent, repost the notice as state law required, and then once the notice expired, file the eviction again and wait for a new court date, which took another month. This small error cost not only the management company but also the property owner. We had to pay twice for a single eviction, which is costly enough, but we also had the apartment occupied for a total of four months without paying rent.

You may think that the address being a little off will not cost the property, but you would be incorrect. The lease shows Mr. Williams apartment as #617, and because we put the notice of nonpayment on the door of #717, once in court, the judge ruled in his favor; it was presumed that we did not post the notice at the correct address. I had to go back and repost a new notice with the correct apartment number, and start the eviction process all over again.

The correct rent and late fees, to me, are the most important things on a lease agreement. If your property charges a one-time late fee, and it is a percentage of the rent, then if you have the rent wrong, the late fee will be incorrect. You may have noticed that Mr. Williams' rent should have been $1,250 per month, which would make the late fee $125 (10 percent of the rent). But the lease shows his rent at $1,050 per month, making the late fee $105. Now you can only charge Mr. Williams $1,050 each month for rent and $105 each month he is late. That is $200 a month less in rent and $20 a month less in late fees. If he has not paid rent, and you sent the notice with $1,250 as the amount of his rent while charging the $125 late fee, then the notice is incorrect. Per the lease agreement signed by both parties, Mr. Williams only owed the property $1,050 per month that he has resided there, and only $105 in late fees for each month he was late. The judge will rule in his favor, and you have to go back to the property and start over again. But this time you will have to credit back $200 each month for the first four months he paid, and $20 each month on the late fee for each of the four months he paid late. If he was late each month, then you would have to credit back $800 in rent and $80 in late fees before his new notice of nonpayment can be issued, and you will not get back the difference.

Due to the above mistake, the new notice of nonpayment of rent was for only $275. That was the difference of the rent credit of $800 (due of the wrong rental amount on the lease of $1,050 per month) and the credit of $80 in late fees (since the signed lease only had a late fee of $105, instead of $125). That leaves the new balance of $170 in rent past due with a $105 late fee, which equals $275.

Resident Not Renewing at End of Lease Term

Now let's discuss what could happen if Mr. Williams was not behind on rent but has decided to move out in the middle of his lease. There are a couple of things that could happen here, because his lease dates are incorrect and the required day of notice is blank. Instead of requiring the sixty-day notice to terminate the lease early, as your property requires, you can only enforce a thirty-day notice from Mr. Williams. That now means that the owners will not receive thirty days of income from Mr. Williams. Those are two easy mistakes that can cost the property to miss out on income.

The lease rent amount was entered incorrectly on the lease, and the reletting fee of $1,062.50 is reduced to $892.50, which is a $170 difference. Now, not only is the property and owner losing out on thirty days of income due to the wrong lease date or the wrong required notice, but now that Mr. Williams is terminating his lease early, and your state allows the reletting fee, the property will earn $170 less in collecting the fee from Mr. Williams. As you can see, the amount of money lost keeps getting higher—all because of small mistakes on the lease agreement.

Resident Is Breaking the Lease Early

Mr. Williams has decided that he wants to purchase a house. He pulls his lease agreement and notices that he only has to pay a $1,250 termination fee, and he only has to give a thirty-day notice. The property now has lost $2,500 if the lease rent was entered correctly at $1,250 a month. Why? If the lease was typed correctly, then Mr. Williams would have to give a sixty-day notice, at $1,250 per month for two months, and $2,500 for two months' rent as termination fee, not just $1,250 for a thirty-day notice and $1,250 for one month's rent as termination fee.

Those are three ways someone may either request or be forced out of a lease agreement. Each one is very important, as you can see. Just one mistake could cause serious setbacks for the property or the owner.

Now that we have covered how incorrect areas of a lease could cost the property or the owner money, let's discuss just some other basic areas of the lease.

Every lease agreement should have a military clause. This would be an area of the lease that will allow active duty military personnel the right to get out of their lease agreement with only a thirty-day notice (even if your property requires a sixty-day notice) and no termination or reletting fees if they go active duty, are deployed, or have military transfer orders. While reading your lease, look for this section and remember it. Something else you should also know about military personnel is that in some states, it is illegal to file an eviction on someone who has been deployed if he has not paid rent. You will need to check with your state laws regarding this. Imagine leaving your apartment or home for vacation or work, only to return and find out all your personal belongings gone. Not a pretty picture, is it?

"Community policies" is a section of a lease agreement that will cover general rules for the community. Some management companies may have their own community policies addendum, and others may use one that is preset for their community with a third party software such as Bluemoon. This addendum will let the residents know the pool regulations, whether you accept packages in the office for residents, and whether you have a business center and the rules for use. You will want to read this addendum to make sure it is accurate, because sometimes rules change. Trust me when I say you will be asked about this on more than one occasion daily.

There is more to the lease than what I have just mentioned, such as additional addendums. Addendums are additions to the lease agreement that pertain to specific rules and city or state requirements. The following are just some additional addendums you may come across:

- gate addendum
- concession addendum
- mold addendum
- garage addendum
- bedbug addendum
- satellite addendum
- utility addendum
- lead hazard information/disclosure addendum(1978)
- asbestos addendum(1981)

The above are only a few additional addendums your property may require. The lead hazard and asbestos addendums are only required based on when your property was built. Each city or state may require some that are specific for your area; you can check with the local apartment association if you have additional questions.

Key Points to Remember

- A lease agreement is a legally binding document.
- Errors on a lease agreement could become costly mistakes to the property or owner.
- Check everything several times before having it signed by either party.
- There are many addendums that could be used at your property.
- Local Apartment Associations are great places to get accurate information about specific addendum's you may be required to use.

Chapter 8

Pre-move-in Inspection

Performing a move-in inspection of the apartment a few days prior to their move-in date is very important. There are many things that could have been overlooked during previous tours, or something could break a day before the move-in day.

To me, it is a good idea to walk a move-in no more than two days prior to the scheduled move-in date. Even though you know that the apartment has been ready for two weeks, and you have even shown the apartment to the new neighbors just last week, many things can go wrong in just a few days. You never know, but a lightbulb could have burned out, the air conditioner could have lost Freon, or a hot-water heater could have burst. These are just a few things that could happen in a few days, so imagine what could happen in a month! If you have not walked the apartment prior to their move-in dates, how would you know about these things? Would you want any of those to be the scenario of your new move-in?

There are several tools you can utilize for a pre-inspection. You could use the same move-in condition form that they will be filling out on move-in day, or even a pre-inspection checklist. If you do not have either of these, simply take a notepad so you are able to write down anything you see that may need repaired. You can find an example move-in inspection checklist in the appendix.

After you have finished your pre-inspection, you should go back to the office and write up any repairs that need to be addressed. Once you have finished writing up the repairs, alert a member of maintenance to what you have found.

If the apartment passed your pre-inspection, then you are set until the move-in date. If you did find items that may need to be repaired, make sure you follow up with the maintenance team to ensure the repairs have been resolved. You will need to walk the apartment again, to make sure it passes your pre-inspection.

If you are unavailable to walk the apartment prior to the scheduled move-in, ask someone to walk it for you. Do not let the first time that you are walking the apartment be with the new neighbors on their move-in day.

Try to put yourself in the mind-set of a new move-in. What do you see that you do not like? I have always gone by this rule of thumb: "Would I live here?" If your answer is no, then it is time to make the repairs needed in order for you to say yes.

Key Points to Remember

- Pre-inspections should be completed no more than two days prior to a move-in date.
- A pre-inspection walk sheet, or the move-in condition form, is a great way to find anything that needs to be repaired prior to a new move-in.
- Anything can happen in an apartment home at any time, so the pre-inspection is very important.
- Never let the first time you are walking an apartment for a new move-in, be with the new neighbors on their move-in day.
- Follow up with the maintenance team to ensure all repairs are completed prior to your new neighbors' move-in.

Chapter 9

Move-In Day

Today is the big day. Today is when all your hard work will pay off. Today is when your lease applicant becomes your resident. Today is their move-in day!

Now that this day has come, are you prepared? Have you pre-walked the apartment to make sure it is ready? Is their move-in packet ready? Do you have their keys and gate remote ready? Is their move-in gift in their apartment, or ready for them to pick up when they arrive? Is their lease printed for their records? These things will be covered in this chapter, so as long as you are following along, then you will be prepared.

Having a perfect move-in day could determine whether tenants will renew their lease when it expires. That's correct: I said renew. You will be surprised how many people will already know, when they move in, whether they will want to renew. A smooth move-in could mean a long-term resident in the future.

Leasing 101 - Garden Style

Moving can be very stressful. Part of your job as a leasing professional is to help reduce their stress. The better organized and prepared you are, the easier and less stressful their move-in will be.

Have you received everything you require from the future residents? Is their lease signed? Do you require renters' insurance or proof of electricity? If you do, did you get these things prior to today? Have you informed the future residents what is left that they need to bring with them? Did you schedule a time for them to come in? Be prepared!

Having everything you need for their file before their move-in day will mean you can quickly get them in and out of the office. Remember that they have many things to do today. They could have movers coming, or helpers who are on a schedule.

Making an appointment for the move-in is a great way to let the guests know you are setting time aside just for them. You will want to make sure that they don't have to wait for you to finish up with another tour. They will know what time will work best for them, so let them tell you. If you are closed for lunch at that time, can you reschedule your lunch? Knowing that they have a set time with you will also be a great time for them to ask you any questions they may have regarding the lease agreement that they may have not spoken to you about before. Did they find errors on the lease? You will now have time to do the corrections without making them wait.

Let's discuss a move-in packet. A move-in packet is great for cross-marketing. Do you have companies you have marketing materials for, and in return, you give your move-ins to them? These are items such as pizza coupons, furniture rentals, cable deals, or alarm companies. This will also be where you have the new residents' printed lease at move-in.

A move-in packet can be a simple pocket folder you create. If your company already has folders, get them ready. The following are just a few things that could be in the move-in packet:

1. Property information sheet
    - Property phone number and address
    - Gate code and instructions
    - Fitness center code
    - After-hours emergency maintenance phone numbers
    - How to contact a courtesy officer after hours
    - Parking instructions (permits, guest parking, towing company)
    - Map of community (showing amenities and mailboxes)
    - School information (Elementary, Middle, and High Schools)
2. Instructions on downloading property app

3. Valet trash instructions (schedule and acceptable trash)
4. Coupons and flyers for local restaurants or stores that you are partnering with for marketing
5. Community newsletter and event flyers for coming up events
6. Cable, internet, and phone providers they are able to use
7. Your business card
8. The signed lease agreement
9. The move-in condition walk sheet
10. Key packet, gate remote (or cards), parking sticker

Does your community use move-in gifts? Move-in gifts could be anything from a basket with snacks in it to what you may have offered as a "look and lease" special (e.g., iPad, TV, radio, or anything tangible). If so, do you have theirs in their apartment, or will it ready for them at their scheduled move-in appointment?

Now that you have everything you need, and your new neighbors know what you need for them to bring with them at move-in, their appointment should be a breeze. Once your appointment arrives, make sure you greet them and welcome them home! Remember: this is time you have set aside for them and only them. For the purpose of this book, we will assume you have everything you need for their completed file and are ready to accept their move-in money and give them their move-in packet.

You have already printed the move-in condition walk sheet for your move-in, so take the time to go with them to their new apartment and help complete the sheet with them. Doing the move-in condition walk sheet with them will ensure that it is completed for your records and theirs, and it will help you find anything in the apartment you may have missed during the pre-move-in inspection.

Once you are at their new home, use the move-in keys to open their door. This is a good way to make sure the keys are cut properly and are in working order. Open the door and let in the new neighbors. Encourage them to walk about and point out anything they may not want to be charged for at move-out, if it was already there at move-in. Is there a spot on the carpet? Is there a small scratch on the countertop? Are there any dents on the appliances? This is a record of the condition of the apartment that they are accepting. These are things that may not be able to be repaired, but they would not want to be charged for if they move out.

As you are completing the move-in condition walk sheet, also make notes of anything that can be repaired. Is there a light out? Is the ice-maker working? Is the toilet running? Items like this will want to be addressed as quickly as possible. These things may not have been visible during your pre-inspection or may have just happened. Assure them that you will have them repaired as quickly as possible. Have a member of the maintenance staff walk with you during the inspection, so he or she can address any issues right then. This will let the new neighbors know that they are important to you.

Now that the walk is complete, it is time to let them move in. Remember: you do not want to take up too much of their time, as they may have a schedule to keep, and you are trying to reduce their stress, not add to it. They have what they need (keys, remotes, parking stickers), and you have what you need. It's time to go back to the office and be prepared for your next appointment, whether it is another move-in or a site tour.

If you did not have a member of maintenance walk with your during the inspection, you will need to make sure you put in any requests for repairs as quickly as possible. Let a member of maintenance know what you or the new neighbors found during the inspection, so they can get the repairs done in a timely manner.

Make sure you follow up with your move-in the next day. Call or e-mail them to see how their move went and ask whether there is anything else that may have come up after you left. Let them know you are there for them.

Key Points to Remember

- Be prepared.
- Have a move-in packet ready with a copy of their signed lease agreement in it.
- Get copies of their IDs, if you have not done so already.
- Be quick but efficient.

Chapter 10

The Resident File

The resident file is a finished product you started when you first answered the phone in the very beginning. I like to compare a resident file to a piece of artwork. This file will be the residents' file for as long as they are with you. Don't you want your team members over the next few years to admire your hard work? I know I do!

Having a perfect resident file is very important for several reasons, which we will cover in this chapter. You will also learn what makes a resident file and how to make it a perfect file.

You will want a perfect resident file that can pass a lease file audit. Many companies perform lease file audits annually or every two years, so you want to make sure your files can pass. Auditors are not there to make you look bad or to make things up to look at; they are there to make sure the property and team members are following company policies, and also to make sure all the information that is in the computer reflects accurately on the lease agreement.

There are many times that a mistake is found on a lease but, for one reason or another, was not corrected at the time the error was found. Auditors will find that error and count off points from your audit score, and then they will make sure that the error is corrected by your office team members by the time the audit is complete. Keep that in mind when you hear, "We are going to be audited next week. Are we ready?" If you follow these guidelines from this book and combine them with your company policies, then you should have no worries about an audit, because you know your files are perfect to the best of your knowledge. I can say that you will also learn something from the outcome of an audit, and it will help you succeed in the future.

Now that I've scared you about the dreaded auditors, let me teach you some ways to help make sure the resident files you create will result in high audit scores.

Because you have already created a perfect applicant file, then you are over half finished. In that chapter you may remember there was no place for a copy of their ID. Well, since you made a copy at move-in, you are ready to place it on the left side of the file. It's best if it is placed as the very first page, behind all other documents on the left side. You will want to be able to find the copy of the IDs quickly if you are ever requested to present it. You never know when you will ever need to look at their IDs after they are put in their file, but when you do need them, make sure you can simply grab a file and flip to the back.

This is also the perfect time to place any other required documents at move-in in their file (e.g., proof of renters' insurance, proof of electric, copies of move-in keys and remotes). Follow your company policy on what side to place those items. I have always placed the proof of electricity, copies of the move-in keys, and remotes on the left side, just behind the application. For proof of renters' insurance, I find is better placed on the right side with the complete lease and all addendums. More than likely, if you require renters' insurance, you will have a renters' insurance addendum, so place the renters' insurance document in front of the addendum.

The order of the lease and addendums should be placed in order of importance. As a manager, when I receive a completed resident file for the final audit and my signing of the lease, the order of the lease and addendums that I like to see the right side of the resident file are as follows:

1. Concession addendum
2. The actual lease agreement
3. Pet addendum (if applicable)

4. Renters' insurance and documentation
5. Community policies
6. Rules and regulations
7. And so on ...
8. The final page should be the completed move-in condition walk sheet with all the notes made by the new neighbor

The reason I prefer this order is simple: I can audit that file quickly, without having to continuously search for the most important parts of the lease agreement, which is how much money will they owe you at the first of each month.

Congratulations! You have now converted an applicant file to a resident file, and it's time to pass the file to the appropriate person to do the final review and approval of the file. This person could be either a leasing manager, assistant manager, or even the business manager. Find out from your team members who would be next.

Keep in mind that the person who is in charge of reviewing the resident file for the final approval may find errors, so be prepared to make corrections—unless you have mastered how to make the perfect resident file!

Additional Notes
The Final Review for Approval

As a manager, I like to do the final review of a resident file, but only after the assistant manager has had time to review it first. Not only can the leasing professional make mistakes, but an assistant manager can also overlook them. To me, having assistant managers review first helps them learn from their own mistakes or oversights, as well as the leasing professionals.

If the property is offering free rent (concessions) or reduced rates, a concession addendum should be used to break down how much they are going to receive as the concession, either up front or as a monthly discount. I want to make sure what was offered to them matches what we say we gave then in the computer.

I can flip to the next page, the lease agreement, because that is what I will need to review to make sure their names are spelled correctly, as well as the lease dates, the rent amounts (before concession), and their deposit amount. I also check that all occupants (those under the legal age to rent in your state, or whoever will be living there that will not be responsible for the apartment; check with your company policies regarding occupants) are all correct on the lease agreement, as well as in the computer.

If the new neighbor has a pet, then the pet addendum should be next. The pet addendum will have what amount they paid for a pet deposit and/or pet fee, as well as if they are going to be paying pet rent per month (check with your community and company policies regarding pets). Exceptions to the pet policies would be service, or companion, animals. Review the Americans with Disabilities Act if you are unsure of what these types of animals are and what forms you may need to show proof of what service the animal may provide to the new neighbor.

Now that you know what they are going to be charged each month per the lease agreement and addendums, and if they match what was input into the computer software, then the other addendums can go in any order, except the very last page (or bottom page), which should always be the completed move-in condition walk sheet, signed by the new neighbors and the leasing professional.

As I mentioned before, to me, these are the most important sections of a lease agreement because they pertain to the income the property will make from this new neighbor per month.

Leasing 101 - Garden Style

Key Points to Remember

- The resident file should be able to pass an audit.
- This will be their resident file for as long as they are your residents, so make it perfect.
- Make sure you arrange all the files the same way each time.
- Service, or companion, animals are an exception to the rules of pets on a property.

Chapter 11

Time to Close

Now that the day is coming to an end, what do you do to get ready to close the office? Do you stop having tours thirty minutes before closing time? Are you all locked up and ready to leave at exactly closing time? If you said yes, then you may get the most out of this chapter.

Most communities are open from 9:00 a.m. to 6:00 p.m., Monday through Friday; weekend hours may vary. The most common hours for an average business are from 9:00 a.m. to 5:00 p.m., which means someone working during the average business hours may only have one hour to look for an apartment. If guests showed up at your office at 5:45 p.m., would you offer to give them a tour, or would you say you stopped touring at 5:30 p.m.? I would certainly offer to give them a tour. The only times I would not tour an apartment would be if I could not make it back to the office before it was dark outside, or if I felt threatened by the guest. My rule of thumb is if someone can make it to my office before I am closed, and I can complete a tour before it is dark outside, then we are going on a tour!

Think of it this way: if you have to go close down the model or show apartments, then why wouldn't you take along someone to tour? You would be able to have a perfect tour and close the show homes at the same time.

Now that all the tours are done for the day, you can start closing the office. In chapter 1, you found a sample opening checklist. If your company does not have a closing checklist, you can always create one. Here are just a few things you should do during the closing process:

1. Make sure all traffic has been entered into the computer for the day.
2. Make sure all phone calls and e-mails have been returned.
3. Make sure all the keys are accounted for.
4. All applicant and resident files should be in a secure lock location (do not leave any files on or in a desk).
5. Are all the TVs, radios, appliances (i.e. coffee maker) turned off?

6. If you have an answering service, do you have to forward the phones?
7. All models and show apartment homes should be locked up with the power turned off.
8. Turn off the office lights.
9. Make sure all the office doors and windows are locked.
10. Turn on the alarm.
11. If you use a golf cart, ensure it has been put away and is charging.

This may seem like a lot to do for closing, but most of the time it takes less than twenty minutes to close up. This is the reason I will take a guest on a tour all the way up until closing is upon me.

Giving that extra time to guests may be the reason they come back and lease from you. You may have been the only community that would offer them a tour in the hour they were off work. That leaves a very nice first impression with them as they drive home to think about where they will be leasing next. I bet it will be with you!

Leasing 101 - Garden Style

Key Points to Remember

- Show the model, or show homes, until your actual closing time. (Or unless it will be dark before you can finish the tour)
- All the traffic for the day should be entered into the computer software before you leave.
- All resident keys should be checked in and accounted for before you leave.
- All resident or applicant files should be placed in a locked area.
- Models and show homes should be closed before you leave. That means turning off the lights, locking the doors, and setting the alarm.

Chapter 12

Review

Now that you have completed Leasing 101, you should have more of an understanding of the Multifamily Housing Industry. As you have read, I bet you discovered there is more to leasing an apartment than you imagined. The Multifamily Housing Industry is an amazing career! I hope that these tools will help you to become the best Leasing and Marketing Professional in the industry.

We have gone over what time to get to work, answering a phone, performing a perfect tour, taking an application, making a resident file, and even closing up for the day. The keys to being a success in this industry are here for you to use as a guide. Never stop looking for new ways to improve your abilities. One of the best things about my career choice was knowing that every day was going to be different from the one before, as well as the ones to come.

Remember, you are on the largest stage with the company you work with. Make sure you use the full stage to show what you can do. You never know who will be watching!

***

Now that you know how to be a Leasing and Marketing Professional, I want to take a moment to mention another important area of the Multifamily Housing Industry. This area is the National Apartment Association and your local Apartment Association.

In many of these chapters you saw I mentioned your local Apartment Association, or the NAA. These associations are there for you. Not only do many of them have Educational Conferences and Trade Shows, which are great ways to receive Continuing Education Credits needed for most Real-estate Licenses, but also for any Designation you receive from the NAA. These trade shows are also a great way to meet new vendors. Some states may combine their local Educational Conference with their State Conference, due to being a smaller association, but they are both amazing to attend.

Your Apartment Associations are also a place for you to become of something more. You can join different committees, such as the Education, Law, Awards, New Members and Vendors, some may have more or less, but they are a very important of our Industry. Reach out to them to find out how you can volunteer for a committee, or to attend their events, just become involved.

There are other ways to be involved, if you do not have spare time. If you have a vendor, or have one that wants to work on your community, ask them if they are members of your Apartment Association. If they are not members, give them your local Apartment Association's phone number, or website, and explain some of the benefits of becoming a member are for them. It's that easy.

Another way to be involved and better your career, is to sign up for one of the educational classes, such as the NALP (National Apartment Leasing Professional) or CAM (Certified Apartment Manager) designations. There are many other classes they offer, not only for the office team members, but for maintenance team members and even vendors.

The importance of supporting and helping your association is because they are the ones that are fighting in the background on legal issues regarding the lease agreement, new laws, and new addenda's. Without support from the communities, their employees, and even vendors, they would be limited on what they would be able to do for our industry. Again, there are many easy ways to get involved with your Apartment Association, find out how you can make a difference.

Leasing 101 - Garden Style

Appendix

Examples

Leasing 101 - Garden Style

Sample Price Sheet

Property Logo or Property Name

Layouts

1 Bedroom 1 Bath	Rates
560 sqft	$0.00 - $0.00
660 sqft	$0.00 - $0.00

1 Bedroom 1 Den 1.5 Bath	
750 sqft	$0.00 - $0.00

2 Bedroom 2 Bath	
865 sqft	$0.00 - $0.00

Application Fee	$0	$XX for guarantor
Reservation Fee	$0	Due at time of lease to hold apartment
Deposit	$0	(Refundable or Non-Refundable)
Valet Trash	$0	Per month
Pet Fee-NF	$0	2 Pet Max with ___ lbs combined weight
Pet Deposit-R	$0	
Pet Rent	$0.00	Breed Restrictions apply; No Aggressive Breeds
Short Term Fee	$0	Per month on any lease between 3-5 months
	$0	Per month on any lease between 6-9 months
Specials as of:	Date Of Speicals	___ months is shortest lease offered

Application approvals are based on income, criminal background checks and credit check.
Anyone over the age of 18 that will be living in the apartment are required to fill out their
own application and be approved.
Occupancy Standards are ____ persons per bedroom.
Prices vary on floor level and availability.
Guarantors for Full Time Students ONLY.
All residents are must have $XXX,XXX in Liability Insurance for apartment.
Applicants must make ___ times their rent as income. (2.5x's or 3x's)
Residents are Responsible for all utilities.

Property Address, Phone Number, Website

Robert Starnes

Open and Closing Checklist

DATE: _____
<u>Opening Checklist</u>

_____Turn alarm off

_____Turn on all lights

_____Check messages

_____Take phones off Service

_____Check Drop Box

_____Set up Refreshment Bar (cookies, coffee, lemonade, ice, cups, napkins)

_____Unlock golf cart

_____Open Business Center

_____Walk through Fitness Center and pick up any trash

_____Walk through pool area and make sure there is no trash and straighten up pool furniture

_____Turn lights on in model

_____Make sure entrances, common areas, and dumpster areas are clean

_____Brochures are stocked

_____Pricing and availability is printed

<u>Closing Checklist</u>

_____Enter all traffic from the day

_____All phone calls and emails are returned

_____Check all keys back into Key System

_____All resident files are in a locked cabinet

_____Turn model lights off

_____Lock up golf cart

_____Turn off T.V. and electronics

_____Break down Refreshment Bar (empty coffee, clean cookie tray, empty trash)

_____Straighten up Kitchen (put dishes in dishwasher, wipe down countertops)

_____Put phones on Service

_____Turn off lights

_____Set alarm

_____Lock all doors   *****Arrive to Work 15 Minutes Early*****

Phone Card

Leasing Professional
_____

Name _____

_____
Date   _Time_

Phone Number (   )   -
Email Address _____ @ _____ .

Preferred way of contact   Phone   Email

How they hear about you   _____

When are they looking to move in   _____

What size apt looking for   _____

Did you have a budget you wanted to stay within   _____

How many people will be staying in the apartment home   _____

How many over the age of 18
(age depends on state and company)   _____

Are you bringing any pets with you   Yes   No   _____

Do you have a floor preferance   Y/N   _____
(1st, 2nd, 3rd)

Anything specific you are looking for in your next apt home   _____
(W/D, Wood Floors, Large walk in closets, Granite Counters)   _____

Have you been able to look at our website   Yes   No   _____

Did you discribe your property amenities
_(BBQ Grills, Pool/Spa, Fitness Center, Limited Access Gates,
Dog Park, Pay Ground) What does your property offer?_

**Did you discuss benefits of living your property or
living on one your management companies properties:**
_(24 hour lock out, 30 day move in guaranty, 24 hour
emergency maint)_

Did you discuss the area? _(Places to eat, schools nearby,
local attrations, how far from Down Town, Malls)_

Do they need directions?

Appointment to view: Date _____   **Time** _____

INCOME CALCULATIONS SHEET

*Examples include sample percentage. <u>Use the percentage required by your community.</u>

Percent required by your community: __33%__

Hourly
Example
$15 per hour x (# of hours worked) = $450 weekly
$450 x 4.33 = $1948.50 monthly
$1,948.50 x .35* (percentage required by community = $681.98 is the rent client qualifies for

___ x ___ (# of hrs worked) =	$0.00	weekly
$0.00 x 4.33 = $0.00 monthly		
$0.00 x 33% (percentage required) =	$0.00	

Weekly
Example
$500 per week x 4.33 = $2,165 monthly
$2,165 x .35* (percentage required by community) = $757.75 is the rent client qualifies for

| ___ x 4.33 = | $0.00 | monthly |
| $0.00 x 33% (percentage required) = | $0.00 | |

Bi-Weekly (client is paid every two weeks / 26 pay periods per year. Typically 80 hours.)
Example
$1,200 per pay period
$1,200 ÷ 2 = $600 weekly
$600 x 4.33 = $2,598 monthly
$2,598 x .35* (percentage required by community) = 909.30 is the rent client qualifies for

___ ÷ 2 =	$0.00	weekly
$0.00 x 4.33	$0.00	monthly
$0.00 x 33% (percentage required) =	$0.00	

Semi-Monthly (Client is paid twice per month / 24 pay periods per year. Typically 86.67 hours.)
Example
$1,200 per pay period
$1,200 x 2 = $2,400 monthly
$2,400 x .35* (percentage required by community) = $840 is the rent client qualifies for

| ___ x 2 = | $0.00 | monthly |
| $0.00 x 33% (percentage required) = | $0.00 | |

Monthly
Example
$1,500 monthly
$1,500 x .35* (percentage required by community) = 525.00 is the rent client qualifies for

| ___ monthly | | |
| $0.00 x 33% (percentage required) = | $0.00 | |

Annually
Example
$60,000 ÷ 12 months = $5,000 monthly
$5,000 x .35% (percentage required by community) = $1,750 is the rent client qualifies for

| ___ ÷ 12 = | $0.00 | monthly |
| $0.00 x 33% (percentage required) = | $0.00 | |

Bank Statement
Example
$900 monthly rent, 12 month lease term
$900 x 12 = 10,800 required in the bank account
$900 ÷ .35 (percentage required by community) = $2,571.43 is the income used for applicant screening

| ___ x 12 (lease term) = | $0.00 | required in bank account |
| $0.00 ÷ 33% (percentage required) = | $0.00 | |

Year-to-Date (Example is assuming that the client has been working since Jan. 1, 2013
Example
$25,000 year to date amount, 4/8/13 pay period end date
98 (# of days from start to pay period end date) ÷ 7 = 14 weeks
$25,000 ÷ 14 weeks = $1,785.71 weekly
$1,785.71 x 4.33 = $7,732.14 monthly
$7,732.14 x .35% (percentage required by community) = $2,706.25 is the rent client qualifies for

	pay period end date		
# of days	0 ÷ 7 =	0	# of weeks
	÷ 0 (# of weeks) =	#DIV/0!	
	#DIV/0! x 4.33	#DIV/0!	monthly
	#DIV/0! x 33% (percentage required) =	#DIV/0!	

Resident's Name: _____   Apt. #: _____   Date: _____

Calculations are correct. Required initials - Manager _____   on-site employee _____

Revised 12/2012

Weekly Income

Weekly

Example
$500 per week x 4.33 = $2165 monthly
$2165 x .35* (percentage required by community) =
$757.75 is the rent client qualifies for

| | x | 4.33 = | $0.00 | |
| $0.00 | x | 0.33 (% required) = | | $0.00 |

Hourly Income

Hourly

Example
$15 per hour x (# of hours worked) = $450 weekly
$450 x 4.33 = $1948.50 monthly
$1948.50 x .35* (percentage required by community) =
$681.98 is the rent client qualifies for

	x	40 (# of hours worked) =		$0.00
$0.00	x	4.33 =	$0.00 monthly	
$0.00	x	0.33 (percentage required) =		$0.00

Robert Starnes

Welcome Letter

WELCOME HOME !!

Applicant(s): _____

_____

Apt. # _____   Move-In Date: _____

Your New Address: New Address _____

City, State Zip Code _____

Will you be bringing a pet(s) with you to your new home?   Yes _____   No _____

Lease Information & Monthly Fees:			Fees and Deposits:		
Lease Begin Date:	_____		Application Fee:	$0.00	Non-Refundable
Lease Term:	_____	Months	Security Deposit:	$0.00	Refundable
Rental Amount:	$0.00	Market	Sure Deposit:	$0.00	One Time Fee
	$0.00	Valet Trash	Admin Fee:	$0.00	Non-Refundable
	$0.00	Short Term Fee	Pet Fee:	$0.00	Non-Refundable
	$0.00	Other	Prorated Rent:	$0.00	
	$0.00	Monthly Charge	Rent Per Day:	$0.00	0 days

Total Due @ Move-In:	$0.00		
	1	$0.00	Prorate
	1	$0.00	Deposit
	1	$0.00	Pet Deposit

Move-In Special:
What are they receiving as a special? Type it out here so
everyone understands if they pull the Welcome Letter.
*(Resident receiving $300 Look and Lease special to be used
in June, making Junes rent $Rent - $300 = $New Rate)*
Utility Account Numer: _____
Renters Insurance Number: _____
_____
_____
_____

NOTES:

> ******No keys will be issued without proof of Utilities in your name upon move-in. There will be no exceptions to the rule. Utility services reverting back to the property after move-in will result in immediate disconnection and a fee of $XX.XX, along with all charges incurred, will be assessed to your account. *After 48 hours, the Admin Fee is no longer refundable* . Please note all terms and conditions are subject to change and/or cancellation without further notice. All application criteria must be met in order for full approval to be issued.******

Applicant is not *guaranteed* a specific apartment. The apartment listed above may change at any time prior to execution of the lease at Management's discretion.

For your convenience, you can log on to **website** to sign up for your utilities.
Electric: Preferred Provider and Phone Number
Phone/Internet: Preferred Provider and Phone Number or Property Rep
Cable: Preferred Provider and Phone Number or Property Rep
Water - Do they set up or do you?
Renter's Insurance: Do you require it? Preferred Provider and Phone Number

Applicant Signature: _____   Lease Date: _____

Applicant Signature: _____   Leased By: _____

Agent's Signature: _____   Date: _____

Leasing 101 - Garden Style

Written Log

				Follow Up Log					
DATE	TIME	GUEST NAME	PHONE OR E-MAIL	GUEST NEEDS AND WANTS	1ST	2ND	3RD	4TH	FINAL

Daily Planner

June — Traffic Follow Up

MONDAY	TUESDAY	WEDNESDAY	THURSDAY	FRIDAY	SATURDAY	SUNDAY
30	31	01	02	03	04	05
06	07	08	09 Email John Williams 1 month follow up.	10 Call Jennifer Jones to follow up for her move in date of 7/1/16.	11	12
13	14	15	16	17	18	19
20	21	22	23 Shonda is looking for 3 weeks, let her know what you have available	24	25	26
27	28	29	30	01	02	03
04	05	Notes:				

Pre-Inspection Checklist

COMMUNITY:

Name		Date		
	Room			
	Front Door	Working	Not Working	Repairs
	Front Door Keys Work			
	All Front Door Locks Work			
	Peep Hole Clear			
	Foyer Lights Working			
	Exterior Light Working			
	Living Room	Working	Not Working	Repairs
	Ceiling Fan			
	Lights			
	Wall Outlets			
	Windows Lock			
	Patio Door Locks			
	Window/Patio Door Blinds			
	Dining Room	Working	Not Working	Repairs
	Dining Room Lights			
	Dining Room Outlets			
	Kitchen			
	Appliances Work:	Working	Not Working	Repairs
	Stove/Oven			
	Stove Vent			
	Microwave			
	Dish Washer			
	Refridgerator/Ice Maker			
	Garbage Disposal			
	Sink/Faucet			
	Sink Stopper			
	Under Kitchen Sink Dry/Leaks			
	Cabinets Cleaned			
	Light Working			
	Clean			
	Bedroom 1	Working	Not Working	Repairs
	Lights			
	Ceiling Fan			
	Window Lock and Screens			
	Blinds			
	Closet shelves			
	Outlets			

Leasing 101 - Garden Style

About the Author

Robert Starnes is the author of The Multifamily Housing Guide – Leasing 101, Garden Style Edition, published 2016. It was the first in a series dedicated to the Multifamily Housing Industry professionals. He, himself, has dedicated almost two decades to the industry and wanted to make sure anyone that is looking to begin a career, his first career passion, have all the tools they need to succeed as he has. Now he has updated his original version with new developments, just from the past two years, for this Anniversary Edition.

Robert now also writes a History Fiction series, *Saving History Series,* which includes *Time Keeper* and *School Bound.* He was born in Texas, but now does most of his writing in Alabama. To learn more about him and his books, visit starnesbooksllc.com, or follow @Starnes_Books on twitter, and find starnesbooksllc on Instagram.

Leasing 101 - Garden Style

Books by Robert Starnes

The Multifamily Housing Guide – Leasing 101 Garden Style Edition – Lulu's publishing (2016)(retired print)

Saving History Series:
Time Keeper – Starnes Books LLC (2018)
School Bound – Starnes Books LLC (2019)

Leasing 101 - Garden Style

Robert Starnes

Leasing 101 - Garden Style

www.ingramcontent.com/pod-product-compliance
Lightning Source LLC
Chambersburg PA
CBHW030258030426
42336CB00009B/425